kid's Animal Pillows

by **Tara Cousins**

LEISURE ARTS, INC. • Maumelle, Arkansas

the Team

Editorial Staff

Senior Product Director: Pam Stebbins
Creative Art Director: Katherine Laughlin
Technical Writer/Editor: Cathy Hardy
Technical Editors: Linda A. Daley, Sarah J. Green, and Lois J. Long
Editorial Writer: Susan Frantz Wiles
Art Category Manager: Lora Puls
Graphic Artist: Jessica Bramlett
Prepress Technician: Stephanie Johnson
Contributing Photographer: Jason Masters
Contributing Photo Stylist: Lori Wenger

Business Staff

President and Chief Executive Officer: Fred F. Pruss
Senior Vice President of Operations: Jim Dittrich
Vice President of Retail Sales: Martha Adams
Chief Financial Officer: Tiffany P. Childers
Controller: Teresa Eby
Information Technology Director: Brian Roden
Director of E-Commerce: Mark Hawkins
Manager of E-Commerce: Robert Young

ISBN-13/EAN: 978-1-4647-3904-0

Look for the camera in our instructions & watch our technique videos made just for you! @ www.leisurearts.com/6581

Meet Tara Cousins

"Hooked" on crochet since the age of 10, Tara Cousins enjoys specializing in children's projects that are fun and functional. "Bright, bold colors and 'picture' patterns are my signature style," she says. Her two young children provide constant inspiration, as well as her desire to make gifts for family and friends. For more about Tara, visit her website, CuteKidsCrochet.com, or her Etsy shop, 3 Little Lambs Crochet. Her first book with Leisure Arts was *Modern Nursery Blankets* (#6237).

Contents

Fox

▰▰▭▭ **EASY**

Finished Size:
12" x 16" (30.5 cm x 40.5 cm)

Shopping List

Yarn (Medium Weight)

[7 ounces, 370 yards
(198 grams, 338 meters) per skein]:

- ☐ Orange - 1 skein
- ☐ Aran - 50 yards (45.5 meters)
- ☐ Brown - small amount
- ☐ Tan - small amount
- ☐ Maroon - small amount

Crochet Hooks

- ☐ Size I (5.5 mm) **and**
- ☐ Size J (6 mm)
  or sizes needed for gauge

Additional Supplies

- ☐ Pillow form - 12" x 16"
  (30.5 cm x 40.5 cm)
- ☐ Yarn needle

GAUGE INFORMATION

The pillow Head, Body, and Tail are worked with the larger size hook. All other pieces are worked with the smaller size hook.

With larger size hook,
   11 sc and 13 rows = 4" (10 cm)
Gauge Swatch: 4" (10 cm) square
With larger size hook and Orange, ch 12.

Row 1: Sc in second ch from hook and in each ch across: 11 sc.
Rows 2-13: Ch 1, turn; sc in each sc across.
Finish off.

——— STITCH GUIDE ———

🎥 TREBLE CROCHET
   (abbreviated tr)

YO twice, insert hook in st indicated, YO and pull up a loop (4 loops on hook), (YO and draw through 2 loops on hook) 3 times.

🎥 SINGLE CROCHET 2 TOGETHER
   (abbreviated sc2tog) (uses 2 sc)

Pull up a loop in each of next 2 sc, YO and draw through all 3 loops on hook (**counts as one sc**).

INSTRUCTIONS

The Head is worked up the front of the pillow, then down the back. The Body is worked across the remaining width of the front and the back, then the last row is joined to the end of rows of the Head.

HEAD

Wind Aran into a small ball, approximately 6 yards (5.5 meters), to be used on Rows 10-16.
Wind Orange into a small ball, approximately 4 yards (3.5 meters), to be used on Rows 10-16 and Rows 26-28. This will prevent the unused yarn from being carried across the row.

With larger size hook and using the larger ball of Aran, ch 20.

Row 1: Sc in second ch from hook and in each ch across: 19 sc.

Row 2 (Right side)**:** Ch 1, turn; sc in each sc across.

Note: Loop a short piece of yarn around any stitch to mark Row 2 as **right** side.

Rows 3-9: Ch 1, turn; sc in each sc across.

Row 10: Ch 1, turn; sc in first 8 sc, sc in next sc 🎥 changing colors *(Figs. 5a & b, page 47)* to the small ball of Orange, do **not** cut unused colors, sc in next sc changing to the small ball of Aran, sc in next 8 sc, sc in last sc changing to the skein of Orange.

Continue to change colors in same manner throughout.

Row 11: Ch 1, turn; sc in first sc changing to Aran, sc in next 8 sc changing to Orange, sc in next sc changing to Aran, sc in last 9 sc.

Row 12: Ch 1, turn; sc in first 9 sc changing to Orange, sc in next 2 sc changing to Aran, sc in next 7 sc changing to Orange, sc in last sc.

Row 13: Ch 1, turn; sc in first 2 sc changing to Aran, sc in next 6 sc changing to Orange, sc in next 2 sc changing to Aran, sc in last 9 sc.

Row 14: Ch 1, turn; sc in first 9 sc changing to Orange, sc in next 3 sc changing to Aran, sc in next 5 sc changing to Orange, sc in last 2 sc.

Row 15: Ch 1, turn; sc in first 2 sc changing to Aran, sc in next 4 sc changing to Orange, sc in next 4 sc changing to Aran, sc in last 9 sc.

Row 16: Ch 1, turn; sc in first 9 sc changing to Orange, sc in next 5 sc changing to Aran, cut small ball of Orange, sc in next 2 sc changing to Orange, cut small ball of Aran, sc in last 3 sc.

Row 17: Ch 1, turn; sc in first 10 sc changing to Aran, sc in last 9 sc.

Row 18: Ch 1, turn; sc in first 9 sc changing to Orange, sc in last 10 sc.

Rows 19-24: Repeat Rows 17 and 18, 3 times.

Row 25: Ch 1, turn; sc in first 10 sc changing to Aran, sc in last 9 sc changing to a small ball of Orange.

5

Row 26: Ch 1, turn; sc in first sc changing to Aran, sc in next 7 sc changing to Orange, sc in last 11 sc.

Row 27: Ch 1, turn; sc in first 11 sc changing to Aran, sc in next 7 sc changing to Orange, sc in last sc.

Row 28: Ch 1, turn; sc in first 3 sc changing to Aran, cut small ball of Orange, sc in next 3 sc changing to Orange, cut Aran, sc in last 13 sc.

Row 29: Ch 1, turn; sc in each sc across.

Repeat Row 29 until Head measures approximately 26" (66 cm) from beginning ch.

Finish off.

EYE (Make 2)
With smaller size hook and Brown, ch 4; join with slip st to form a ring, finish off leaving a long end for sewing.

NOSE
With smaller size hook and Tan, ch 4; join with slip st to form a ring, finish off leaving a long end for sewing.

FACE ASSEMBLY
Use photo as a guide for placement of all pieces.

Sew the Eyes and Nose to the Head.

Smile: With smaller size hook and Maroon, ch 5; finish off leaving a long end for sewing.

Sew the Smile to the Head.

BODY
With larger size hook and Orange, ch 73.

Row 1: Sc in second ch from hook and in each ch across: 72 sc.

Row 2: Ch 1, turn; sc in each sc across.

Repeat Row 2 until Body measures approximately 10" (25.5 cm) from beginning ch.

Joining Row: Ch 1, turn; place Head in front of Body with **right** side of Head facing you. Working through **both** pieces, in end of rows across Head and in each sc on Body, sc across; finish off.

TAIL
With larger size hook and Aran, ch 10.

Row 1 (Right side): Sc in second ch from hook and in each ch across: 9 sc.

Note: Mark Row 1 as **right** side.

Rows 2 and 3: Ch 1, turn; 2 sc in first sc, sc in each sc across to last sc, 2 sc in last sc: 13 sc.

Row 4: Ch 1, turn; sc in each sc across.

Row 5: Ch 1, turn; 2 sc in first sc, sc in each sc across to last sc, 2 sc in last sc: 15 sc.

Rows 6-8: Ch 1, turn; sc in each sc across.

Finish off leaving a long end for sewing.

Row 9: With **right** side facing, leaving a long end for sewing, and ▶ working in Back Loops Only *(Fig. 4, page 46)*, join Orange with slip st in first sc; ch 1, sc in same st and in each sc across.

Rows 10-12: Ch 1, turn; sc in both loops of each sc across.

Row 13: Ch 1, turn; beginning in first sc, sc2tog, sc in next 11 sc, sc2tog: 13 sc.

Row 14: Ch 1, turn; sc in each sc across.

Row 15: Ch 1, turn; beginning in first sc, sc2tog, sc in next 9 sc, sc2tog: 11 sc.

Rows 16 and 17: Ch 1, turn; sc in each sc across.

Row 18: Ch 1, turn; beginning in first sc, sc2tog, sc in next 7 sc, sc2tog: 9 sc.

Rows 19-22: Ch 1, turn; sc in each sc across.

Row 23: Ch 1, turn; beginning in first sc, sc2tog, sc in next 5 sc, sc2tog: 7 sc.

Rows 24-36: Ch 1, turn; sc in each sc across.

Row 37: Ch 1, turn; beginning in first sc, sc2tog, sc in next 3 sc, sc2tog: 5 sc.

Rows 38-48: Ch 1, turn; sc in each sc across.

Finish off leaving a long end for sewing.

EAR (Make 2)
Make one piece with Aran and one piece with Orange for **each** ear.

With smaller size hook, ch 6.

Row 1: Slip st in second ch from hook, sc in next ch, hdc in next ch, dc in next ch, tr in last ch; finish off leaving a long end for sewing.

Place one Aran piece and one Orange piece together and  whipstitch *(Fig. 6b, page 47)* across the beginning ch and the top of the stitches.

FINISHING
The pillow form may be covered if desired.

Use photos, pages 5 and 7, as guides for placement of all pieces.

Use backstitch *(Fig. 7, page 47)* for the method of sewing to attach the Tail to the Body, leaving the edge of the Tail free.

Fold the Head and Body in half with **wrong** sides together, matching the end of rows on the Body. With the **wrong** side of the Tail facing up, line up the last row with the top fold of the Body, extending one stitch on the right hand side of the Tail over the edge of the Body. Fold the Tail so that the **right** side of the Aran section is facing up with the side edge 1" (2.5 cm) up from the bottom edge.

Using Aran, sew the Aran section of the Tail in place. Using the Orange yarn end left at the color change, sew across the bottom portion of the Tail to the fold. Using the Orange yarn end left at the end of the last row, sew along the top edge and the inside of the Tail, leaving the remaining side edge free.

Flatten the Body; using Orange, whipstitch across the 3 sides, inserting the pillow form before working across the last side.

Sew one Ear to the top of the Head at the side seam and one to the top near the Body.

Lion

◼◼◻◻ **EASY**

Finished Size: 12" x 16"
(30.5 cm x 40.5 cm)

Shopping List

Yarn (Medium Weight) [4]

[7 ounces, 370 yards
(198 grams, 338 meters) per skein]:

- ☐ Gold - 1 skein
- ☐ Orange - 55 yards (50.5 meters)
- ☐ Brown - small amount
- ☐ White - small amount
- ☐ Maroon - small amount

Crochet Hooks

- ☐ Size I (5.5 mm) **and**
- ☐ Size J (6 mm)

  or sizes needed for gauge

Additional Supplies

- ☐ Pillow form - 12" x 16"
  (30.5 cm x 40.5 cm)
- ☐ Yarn needle

GAUGE INFORMATION

The pillow Body is worked with the larger size hook. All other pieces are worked with the smaller size hook.

With larger size hook, in Body pattern,
  12 sts and 8 rows = 3¼" (8.25 cm)
Gauge Swatch: 3¼" (8.25 cm)
  square
With larger size hook and Gold, ch 12.
Work same as Body Rows 1-8: 8 sc and 4 chs.
Finish off.

─── STITCH GUIDE ───

 TREBLE CROCHET
  (abbreviated tr)
YO twice, insert hook in st indicated, YO and pull up a loop (4 loops on hook), (YO and draw through 2 loops on hook) 3 times.

🎥 **SINGLE CROCHET 2 TOGETHER**
  (abbreviated sc2tog) (uses 2 sc)
Pull up a loop in each of next 2 sc, YO and draw through all 3 loops on hook **(counts as one sc).**

─────────────────────

INSTRUCTIONS

BODY (Make 2)

With larger size hook, Gold, and beginning at bottom edge, ch 48.

Row 1: (Sc, ch 1, sc) in third ch from hook, ★ skip next 2 chs, (sc, ch 1, sc) in next ch; repeat from ★ across: 32 sc and 16 chs.

Row 2: Ch 1, turn; skip first sc, (sc, ch 1, sc) in next ch, ★ skip next 2 sc, (sc, ch 1, sc) in next ch; repeat from ★ across to last sc, leave last sc unworked.

Repeat Row 2 for pattern until Body measures approximately 16¼" (41.5 cm) from beginning ch.

Finish off leaving a long end for sewing on only one of the Body pieces.

LEG (Make 4)

Rnd 1 (Right side)**:** With smaller size hook and Gold, 🎥 make an adjustable loop to form a ring **(Figs. 1a-d, page 46)**; 8 sc in ring; join with slip st to first sc.

Rnd 2: Ch 1, 2 sc in same sc as joining, sc in next sc, (2 sc in next sc, sc in next sc) around; join with slip st to first sc: 12 sc.

Rnds 3 and 4: Ch 1, sc in each sc around; join with slip st to first sc.

Rnd 5: Ch 1, sc in same sc as joining, sc2tog, (sc in next sc, sc2tog) around; join with slip st to first sc: 8 sc.

Rnd 6: Ch 1, sc in each sc around; join with slip st to first sc, finish off leaving a long end for sewing.

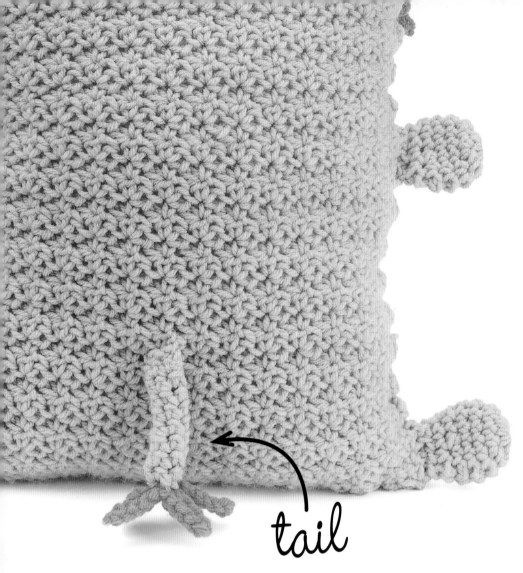

tail

Row 2 (front)**:** Ch 1, turn; sc in first 2 sc, 2 sc in each of next 4 dc, sc in last 2 sc; finish off leaving a long end for sewing: 12 sts.

INNER EAR (Make 2)

Row 1 (front)**:** With smaller size hook and Maroon, make an adjustable loop to form a ring; (2 sc, 3 dc, 2 sc) in ring; do **not** join, finish off leaving a long end for sewing: 7 sts.

NOSE

Row 1 (Right side)**:** With smaller size hook and Brown, ch 4, dc in third ch from hook, tr in last ch; finish off leaving a long end for sewing.

EYE (Make 2)

Rnd 1 (Right side)**:** With smaller size hook and White, make an adjustable loop to form a ring; 9 hdc in ring; join with slip st to first hdc, finish off leaving a long end for sewing.

Pupil: With smaller size hook and Brown, ch 4; join with slip st to form a ring, finish off leaving a long end for sewing.

TAIL

Rnd 1 (Wrong side)**:** With smaller size hook and Gold, make an adjustable loop to form a ring; 5 sc in ring; do **not** join.

Pull the yarn end through ring to front of work. Sc in each sc around, forming a tube and working on the **inside**, until Tail measures approximately 3" (7.5 cm); finish off leaving a long end for sewing.

Working in sts around tip of Tail (beginning end), join Orange with slip st around any st; ch 11, (slip st around next st, ch 11) 4 times; slip st in same st as joining st; finish off.

OUTER EAR (Make 2)

Row 1: With smaller size hook and Gold, make an adjustable loop to form a ring; (2 sc, 4 dc, 2 sc) in ring; do **not** join: 8 sts.

MANE

The Mane is made up of 2 rounds of chain loops worked directly onto one of the Body pieces in an oval shape to form the Head. To serve as a guide for placement of the Outer Rnd, sew a  running stitch *(Fig. 8, page 47)* where the Mane will go, approximately 1½" (4 cm) from the top and side edges and making the oval large enough to fit all of the facial features. The running st will be removed later.

When working a slip st on the Body, be sure to insert your hook under 2 strands for a secure attachment.

Outer Rnd: Using smaller size hook, join Orange with slip st in any st along the outside of the running stitch; ch 10, (slip st on Body, ch 10) around; join with slip st to first slip st, do **not** finish off.

Remove the running stitch.

Inner Rnd: Working in sts inside the Outer Rnd; (slip st on Body, ch 7) around; join with slip st to first slip st, finish off.

FACE ASSEMBLY

Use photo as a guide for placement of all pieces.

Sew each Pupil to the edge of an Eye at the joining.

Smile: With smaller size hook and Maroon, ch 4; finish off leaving a long end for sewing.

Sew the Smile to the Head.

Use backstitch *(Fig. 7, page 47)* for the method of sewing to attach the features to the Body, leaving the edge of each piece free.

Sew the Nose to the Head with the tr at the end of the row at the top.

Sew the Eyes to the Head with the Pupils positioned to the side.

Sew the straight edge of the Outer Ears between the two rounds of the Mane, then sew the Inner Ears in front of them.

FINISHING

The pillow form may be covered if desired.

Flatten the last rnd of the Tail. Working through both layers, whipstitch the Tail to the remaining Body piece *(Figs. 6a & b, page 47)*, placing it diagonally, 4" (10 cm) up from the beginning ch.

Place the Body pieces with **wrong** sides together and the beginning chs at the same end. Whipstitch across each side, inserting the pillow form before working across the last side.

Using photo as a guide for placement, flatten the Legs and sew the last rnd to the Body at the seams.

Owl

◼◼◻◻ **EASY**

Finished Size: 12" x 16"
(30.5 cm x 40.5 cm)

Shopping List

Yarn (Medium Weight)

[7 ounces, 370 yards
(198 grams, 338 meters) per skein]:

☐ Tan - 1 skein
☐ Blue - 45 yards (41 meters)
☐ Yellow - 35 yards (32 meters)
☐ Orange - small amount
☐ White - small amount
☐ Brown - small amount

Crochet Hooks

☐ Size I (5.5 mm) **and**
☐ Size J (6 mm)
  or sizes needed for gauge

Additional Supplies

☐ Pillow form - 12" x 16"
  (30.5 cm x 40.5 cm)
☐ Yarn needle

GAUGE INFORMATION

With larger size hook, in Body pattern,
  8 sts = 3" (7.5 cm),
  8 rows = 3¼" (8.25 cm)
Gauge Swatch: 3" wide x 3¼" high
  (7.5 cm x 8.25 cm)
With larger size hook and Tan, ch 9.
Work same as Body Rows 1-8: 8 sts.
Finish off.

——— STITCH GUIDE ———

🎥 **TREBLE CROCHET**
    (abbreviated tr)
YO twice, insert hook in st indicated,
YO and pull up a loop (4 loops on
hook), (YO and draw through 2 loops
on hook) 3 times.

🎥 **SINGLE CROCHET 2 TOGETHER**
    (abbreviated sc2tog) (uses 2 sts)
Pull up a loop in each of next 2 sts, YO
and draw through all 3 loops on hook
(counts as one sc).

INSTRUCTIONS
BODY

The Body is worked across the width
of the front and the back. The end of
rows will be joined to form a seam
lengthwise across the center back.

With larger size hook, Tan, and
beginning at bottom edge, ch 73.

Row 1: Sc in second ch from hook, dc
in next ch, (sc in next ch, dc in next
ch) across: 72 sts.

Row 2: Ch 1, turn; sc in first dc, dc in
next sc, (sc in next dc, dc in next sc)
across.

Repeat Row 2 for pattern until Body
measures approximately 16¼"
(41.5 cm) from beginning ch; do **not**
finish off.

Back Seam: Fold the Body piece in
half matching rows. Working
through **both** layers, slip st evenly
across; finish off.

EAR (Make 2)

With larger size hook, Tan, and
leaving a long end for sewing, ch 6.

Row 1: Sc in second ch from hook,
(dc in next ch, sc in next ch) twice:
5 sts.

Row 2: Ch 1, turn; dc in first sc, sc in
next dc, dc in next sc, sc2tog: 4 sts.

Row 3: Ch 1, turn; sc in first 2 sts, dc
in next sc, sc in last dc.

Row 4: Ch 1, turn; dc in first sc, sc in
next dc, sc2tog; finish off: 3 sts.

WING (Make 2)

With larger size hook and Blue, ch 3.

Row 1: Sc in second ch from hook
and in next ch: 2 sc.

Row 2 (Right side)**:** Ch 1, turn; 2 sc in each sc 🎥 changing to Yellow in last sc made *(Fig. 5a, page 47)*; do **not** cut Blue: 4 sc.

Note: Loop a short piece of yarn around any stitch to mark Row 2 as **right** side.

Stripes are formed by alternating two rows of each color. The unused color will be carried along the edge.

Row 3: Ch 1, turn; 2 sc in first sc, sc in next 2 sc, 2 sc in last sc: 6 sc.

Row 4: Ch 1, turn; sc in each sc across changing to Blue in last sc.

Row 5: Ch 1, turn; 2 sc in first sc, sc in each sc across to last sc, 2 sc in last sc: 8 sc.

Row 6: Ch 1, turn; 2 sc in first sc, sc in each sc across to last sc, 2 sc in last sc changing to Yellow in last sc: 10 sc.

Row 7: Ch 1, turn; 2 sc in first sc, sc in each sc across to last sc, 2 sc in last sc: 12 sc.

Row 8: Ch 1, turn; sc in each sc across changing colors in last sc.

Rows 9-12: Repeat Rows 7 and 8 twice: 16 sc.

Row 13: Ch 1, turn; sc in each sc across.

Row 14: Ch 1, turn; sc in each sc across changing colors in last sc.

Rows 15-22: Repeat Rows 13 and 14, 4 times.

Row 23 (Decrease row)**:** Ch 1, turn; beginning in first sc, sc2tog, sc in each sc across to last 2 sc, sc2tog: 14 sc.

Row 24: Ch 1, turn; sc in each sc across changing colors in last sc.

Rows 25-31: Repeat Rows 23 and 24, 3 times; then repeat Row 23 once **more**: 6 sc.

Row 32: Ch 1, turn; beginning in first sc, sc2tog, sc in next 2 sc, sc2tog changing colors; cut Yellow: 4 sc.

Row 33: Ch 1, turn; beginning in first sc, sc2tog twice: 2 sc.

Row 34: Ch 1, turn; sc in each sc across.

Edging: Working in end of rows and 🎥 in free loops of beginning ch *(Fig. 3, page 46)*, slip st evenly around entire Wing; join with slip st to first st, finish off leaving a long end for sewing.

FOOT (Make 2)

With smaller size hook and Orange, ch 8.

Row 1: Sc in second ch from hook and in each ch across: 7 sc.

Row 2 (Toes)**:** Ch 3, turn; skip first sc, tr in next sc, ch 3, slip st in next sc, ★ ch 3, tr in next sc, ch 3, slip st in next sc; repeat from ★ once **more**; finish off leaving a long end for sewing.

BEAK

With smaller size hook and Orange, ch 5.

Row 1: 🎥 Working in back ridge of chs *(Fig. 2, page 46)*, slip st in second ch from hook, sc in next ch, dc in next ch, tr in last ch; finish off leaving a long end for sewing.

EYE (Make 2)

With smaller size hook and Tan, ch 6.

Row 1: Sc in second ch from hook and in each ch across: 5 sc.

Row 2 (Right side)**:** Ch 1, turn; 2 sc in first sc, sc in next 3 sc, 2 sc in last sc: 7 sc.

Note: Mark Row 2 as **right** side.

Row 3: Ch 1, turn; sc in each sc across.

Row 4: Ch 1, turn; 2 sc in first sc, sc in next 5 sc, 2 sc in last sc: 9 sc.

Row 5: Ch 1, turn; sc in each sc across to last sc; leaving a long end for sewing on both Tan and White, sc in last sc changing to White, then cut Tan.

Row 6: Ch 1, turn; 🎥 working in Back Loops Only *(Fig. 4, page 46)*, sc in each sc across.

Row 7: Ch 1, turn; sc in both loops of each sc across.

Rows 8-10: Ch 1, turn; beginning in first sc, sc2tog, sc in each sc across to last 2 sc, sc2tog: 3 sc.

Finish off.

Pupil: With Brown, ch 4; join with slip st to form a ring, finish off leaving a long end for sewing.

FACE ASSEMBLY

Use photo as a guide for placement of all pieces.

Use 🎥 backstitch *(Fig. 7, page 47)* for the method of sewing to attach the features to the Body, leaving the edge of each piece free.

Sew each Pupil to the bottom of the White section of an Eye, positioned slightly to one side.

Flatten the Body with the seam at the side edge and mark the top and bottom edges of the fold to indicate the center front.

Move the seam to the center back. Using the markers as a guide, place the Eyes on the front of the Body, beginning 3¹⁄₂" (9 cm) down from the top edge; sew in place using the matching yarn ends.

Sew the Beak between the Eyes with the tr at the end of the row at the top.

FINISHING

The pillow form may be covered if desired.

Flatten the Body placing the seam and bottom marker together; 🎥 whipstitch across the bottom edge *(Fig. 6a, page 47)*.

The pillow form can be temporarily inserted in the Body to make placement of the Wings easier. Sew the Wings to the Body, wrapping them around the sides.

Sew Row 1 of each Foot to the bottom of the Body leaving the toes free.

Remove the pillow form to weave in the yarn ends.

Insert the pillow form. Flatten the top edge of the Body placing the seam and top marker together, then whipstitch across the top edge.

Sew the beginning ch of the Ears to the top seam of the Body, placing the decreased edges facing toward the center.

15

Monkey

■■□□ EASY

Finished Size: 12" x 16"
(30.5 cm x 40.5 cm)

Shopping List

Yarn (Medium Weight)

[7 ounces, 370 yards
(198 grams, 338 meters) per skein]:

☐ Brown - 1 skein
☐ Tan - 40 yards (36.5 meters)
☐ Rose - small amount
☐ White - small amount
☐ Black - small amount

Crochet Hooks

☐ Size I (5.5 mm) **and**
☐ Size J (6 mm)
or sizes needed for gauge

Additional Supplies

☐ Pillow form - 12" x 16"
(30.5 cm x 40.5 cm)
☐ Yarn needle

GAUGE INFORMATION

The pillow Body is worked with the larger size hook. All other pieces are worked with the smaller size hook.

With larger size hook, in Body pattern, 12 sts and 8 rows = 4" (10 cm)

Gauge Swatch: 4" (10 cm) square

With larger size hook and Brown, ch 13.

Work same as Body Rows 1-8: 12 sts. Finish off.

STITCH GUIDE

🎥 FRONT POST DOUBLE CROCHET (abbreviated FPdc)

YO, insert hook from **front** to **back** around post of st indicated (**Fig. A**), YO and pull up a loop (3 loops on hook) (**Fig. B**), (YO and draw through 2 loops on hook) twice.

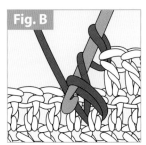

🎥 BACK POST DOUBLE CROCHET (abbreviated BPdc)

YO, insert hook from **back** to **front** around post of st indicated (**Fig. C**), YO and pull up a loop (3 loops on hook) (**Fig. D**), (YO and draw through 2 loops on hook) twice.

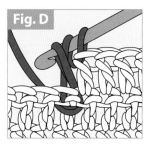

🎥 SINGLE CROCHET 2 TOGETHER (abbreviated sc2tog) (uses 2 sc)

Pull up a loop in each of next 2 sc, YO and draw through all 3 loops on hook (**counts as one sc**).

INSTRUCTIONS

The Body is worked across the width of the front and the back. The end of rows will be joined to form a seam lengthwise across the center back.

BODY

With larger size hook, Brown, and beginning at bottom edge, ch 79.

Row 1: Dc in third ch from hook **(2 skipped chs count as first dc)** and in each ch across: 78 dc.

Row 2: Ch 2 **(counts as first dc, now and throughout)**, turn; work (FPdc around next st, BPdc around next st) across to last dc, dc in last dc.

Row 3: Ch 2, turn; work (BPdc around next st, FPdc around next st) across to last dc, dc in last dc.

Repeat Rows 2 and 3 for pattern until Body measures approximately 16¼" (41.5 cm) from beginning ch.

Finish off leaving a long end for sewing.

Back seam: Fold the Body piece in half matching rows. 🎥 Whipstitch across the end of rows *(Fig. 6b, page 47)*.

TAIL

With smaller size hook and Brown, ch 50.

Row 1: 🎥 Working in back ridge of chs *(Fig. 2, page 46)*, dc in third ch from hook and in each ch across; finish off leaving a long end for sewing.

LEG (Make 2)

Rnd 1: With smaller size hook and Brown, 🎥 make an adjustable loop to form a ring *(Figs. 1a-d, page 46)*; 8 sc in ring; do **not** join, 🎥 place a marker to indicate beginning of the rnd *(see Markers, page 46)*.

Rnds 2 and 3: Sc in each sc around.

Slip st in next sc, finish off leaving a long end for sewing.

ARM (Make 2)

Work same as Leg, working 5 rnds.

OUTER EAR (Make 2)

Row 1: With smaller size hook and Brown, make an adjustable loop to form a ring; (2 sc, 4 dc, 2 sc) in ring; do **not** join: 8 sts.

Row 2 (front)**:** Ch 1, turn; sc in first 2 sc, 2 hdc in each of next 4 dc, sc in last 2 sc; finish off leaving a long end for sewing: 12 sts.

INNER EAR (Make 2)

Row 1 (front)**:** With smaller size hook and Rose, make an adjustable loop to form a ring; (2 sc, 3 dc, 2 sc) in ring; do **not** join, finish off leaving a long end for sewing: 7 sts.

Sew the back of each Inner Ear to the front of an Outer Ear.

EYE PATCH

With smaller size hook and Tan, ch 22.

Row 1: Sc in second ch from hook and in each ch across: 21 sc.

Rows 2-6: Ch 1, turn; sc in each sc across.

Row 7: Ch 1, turn; beginning in first sc, sc2tog, sc in each sc across to last 2 sc, sc2tog: 19 sc.

FIRST SIDE

Row 8 (Right side)**:** Ch 1, turn; sc in first 8 sc, sc2tog, leave remaining 9 sc unworked: 9 sc.

Rows 9 and 10: Ch 1, turn; beginning in first sc, sc2tog, sc in each sc across to last 2 sc, sc2tog: 5 sc.

Finish off.

SECOND SIDE

Row 8: With **right** side facing, join Tan with slip st in same st as last st of First Side; beginning in same st, sc2tog, sc in last 8 sc: 9 sc.

Rows 9 and 10: Ch 1, turn; beginning in first sc, sc2tog, sc in each sc across to last 2 sc, sc2tog: 5 sc.

Finish off leaving a long end for sewing.

MUZZLE

With smaller size hook and Tan, ch 13.

Rnd 1 (Right side)**:** 4 Sc in second ch from hook, sc in next 10 chs, 4 sc in last ch; working in free loops of beginning ch *(Fig. 3, page 46)*, sc in next 10 chs; join with slip st to first sc: 28 sc.

Note: Mark Rnd 1 as **right** side.

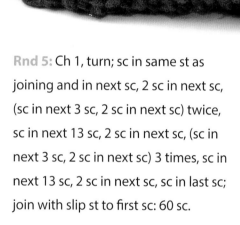

tail

Rnd 2: Ch 1, turn; 2 sc in same st as joining, sc in next 10 sc, 2 sc in each of next 4 sc, sc in next 10 sc, 2 sc in each of last 3 sc; join with slip st to first sc: 36 sc.

Rnd 3: Ch 1, turn; sc in same st as joining, 2 sc in next sc, (sc in next sc, 2 sc in next sc) twice, sc in next 11 sc, 2 sc in next sc, (sc in next sc, 2 sc in next sc) 3 times, sc in next 11 sc, 2 sc in last sc; join with slip st to first sc: 44 sc.

Rnd 4: Ch 1, turn; sc in same st as joining, 2 sc in next sc, sc in next 12 sc, 2 sc in next sc, (sc in next 2 sc, 2 sc in next sc) 3 times, sc in next 12 sc, 2 sc in next sc, (sc in next 2 sc, 2 sc in next sc) twice, sc in last sc; join with slip st to first sc: 52 sc.

Rnd 5: Ch 1, turn; sc in same st as joining and in next sc, 2 sc in next sc, (sc in next 3 sc, 2 sc in next sc) twice, sc in next 13 sc, 2 sc in next sc, (sc in next 3 sc, 2 sc in next sc) 3 times, sc in next 13 sc, 2 sc in next sc, sc in last sc; join with slip st to first sc: 60 sc.

Rnd 6: Ch 1, turn; sc in same st as joining and in next sc, 2 sc in next sc, sc in next 14 sc, 2 sc in next sc, (sc in next 4 sc, 2 sc in next sc) 3 times, sc in next 14 sc, 2 sc in next sc, (sc in next 4 sc, 2 sc in next sc) twice, sc in last 2 sc; join with slip st to first sc: 68 sc.

Rnd 7: Ch 1, turn; sc in each sc around; join with slip st to first sc, finish off leaving a long end for sewing.

NOSE

With smaller size hook and Rose, ch 5.

Row 1: Sc in second ch from hook and in each ch across: 4 sc.

Row 2: Ch 1, turn; beginning in first sc, sc2tog twice: 2 sc.

Row 3: Ch 1, turn; beginning in first sc, sc2tog; finish off leaving a long end for sewing.

EYE (Make 2)

Rnd 1 (Right side)**:** With smaller size hook and White, make an adjustable loop to form a ring; 6 sc in ring; join with slip st to first sc, finish off leaving a long end for sewing.

Pupil: With Black, ch 3; finish off leaving a long end for sewing.

FACE ASSEMBLY

Use photos as a guide for placement of all pieces.

Sew each Pupil to the edge of an Eye at the joining.

Use  backstitch *(Fig. 7, page 47)* for the method of sewing to attach the features to the Body, leaving the edge of each piece free.

Sew the Nose to the center top of the Muzzle with the beginning ch of the Nose at the top.

Smile: With smaller size hook and Brown, ch 6; finish off leaving a long end for sewing.

Sew the Smile to the Muzzle forming a sideways grin.

Sew the Eyes to Rows 4-6 of the Eye Patch, 1" (2.5 cm) apart, with the Pupils positioned to one side.

Flatten the Body with the seam at the side edge and mark the top and bottom edges of the fold to indicate the center of the front.

Move the seam to the center back. Using the markers as a guide, place the Eye Patch on the front of the Body, beginning 2½" (6.5 cm) down from the top edge; sew in place.

Sew the Muzzle to the Body, placing the top edge over the first 2 rows of the Eye Patch.

FINISHING

The pillow form may be covered if desired.

Place the Tail on the back of the Body piece with one end at the beginning ch a few sts from the seam. Curve the Tail, folding it over at the center point. Sew the top of the stitches of the Tail in place.

The pillow form can be temporarily inserted at any time to make placement of pieces easier.

Sew the Arms and Legs to the side of the Body.

Sew the Ears to the Body placing them slightly in from the side edge and the top even with the top of the Eye Patch.

Remove the pillow form to weave in the yarn ends.

Flatten the top edge of the Body placing the seam and top marker together, then whipstitch across the top edge *(Fig. 6a, page 47)*.

Insert the pillow form. Flatten the bottom edge of the Body placing the seam and bottom marker together, then whipstitch across the bottom edge.

Sheep

◼◼◻◻ EASY

Finished Size: 12" x 16"
(30.5 cm x 40.5 cm)
Shown on page 22.

Shopping List

Yarn (Medium Weight)

[7 ounces, 370 yards
(198 grams, 338 meters) per skein]:

- ☐ White - 1 skein
- ☐ Grey - 25 yards (23 meters)
- ☐ Black - small amount
- ☐ Pink - small amount

Crochet Hooks

- ☐ Size I (5.5 mm) **and**
- ☐ Size J (6 mm)
  or sizes needed for gauge

Additional Supplies

- ☐ Pillow form - 12" x 16"
  (30.5 cm x 40.5 cm)
- ☐ Yarn needle

GAUGE INFORMATION

The pillow Front and Back Body are worked with the larger size hook. All other pieces are worked with the smaller size hook.

With larger size hook, in Body pattern,
    8 sts = 3¼" (8.25 cm),
    6 rows = 3" (7.5 cm)
Gauge Swatch: 3½" wide x 3" high
    (9 cm x 7.5 cm)
With larger size hook and White,
ch 10.
Work same as Body Rows 1-6: 9 sts.
Finish off.

—— STITCH GUIDE ——

🎥 **CLUSTER** (uses one sc)
★ YO, insert hook in sc indicated, YO and pull up a loop, YO and draw through 2 loops on hook; repeat from ★ 4 times **more**, YO and draw through all 6 loops on hook.

🎥 **SINGLE CROCHET 2 TOGETHER**
    (abbreviated sc2tog) (uses 2 sc)
Pull up a loop in each of next 2 sc, YO and draw through all 3 loops on hook (**counts as one sc**).

INSTRUCTIONS
FRONT BODY

With larger size hook, White, and beginning at bottom edge, ch 42.

Row 1 (Right side)**:** Sc in second ch from hook and in each ch across: 41 sc.

Note: Loop a short piece of yarn around any stitch to mark Row 1 as **right** side.

Turning ch-2 does **not** count as a st.

Row 2: Ch 2, turn; dc in first sc, (work Cluster in next sc, dc in next sc) across: 20 Clusters and 21 dc.

Row 3: Ch 1, turn; sc in each st across: 41 sc.

Row 4: Ch 2, turn; work Cluster in first sc, (dc in next sc, work Cluster in next sc) across: 21 Clusters and 20 dc.

Row 5: Ch 1, turn; sc in each st across: 41 sc.

Repeat Rows 2-5 for pattern until Body measures approximately 13" (33 cm) from beginning ch, ending by working Row 2.

Finish off.

BACK BODY

With larger size hook, White, and beginning at bottom edge, ch 42.

Row 1 (Right side)**:** Sc in second ch from hook and in each ch across: 41 sc.

Note: Mark Row 1 as **right** side.

Turning ch-2 does **not** count as a st.

Work same as Front Body, beginning and ending by working Row 4.

LEG (Make 2)

Rnd 1 (Right side)**:** With smaller size hook and Grey,  make an adjustable loop to form a ring *(Figs. 1a-d, page 46)*; 6 sc in ring; do **not** join.

Sc in each sc around until Leg measures approximately 1½" (4 cm).

Slip st in next sc, finish off leaving a long end for sewing.

TAIL

With smaller size hook and Grey, ch 10.

Row 1: Sc in second ch from hook, dc in last 8 chs; finish off leaving a long end for sewing.

HEAD

With smaller size hook and Grey, ch 4.

Row 1 (Right side)**:** Sc in second ch from hook and in last 2 chs: 3 sc.

Note: Mark Row 1 as **right** side.

Row 2: Ch 1, turn; 2 sc in first sc, sc in next sc, 2 sc in last sc: 5 sc.

Row 3: Ch 1, turn; sc in each sc across.

Rows 4-6: Ch 1, turn; 2 sc in first sc, sc in each sc across to last sc, 2 sc in last sc: 11 sc.

Rows 7 and 8: Ch 1, turn; sc in each sc across.

Row 9: Ch 1, turn; 2 sc in first sc, sc in each sc across to last sc, 2 sc in last sc: 13 sc.

Rows 10-14: Ch 1, turn; sc in each sc across.

Row 15: Ch 1, turn; beginning in first sc, sc2tog twice, sc in next 5 sc, sc2tog twice: 9 sc.

Row 16: Ch 1, turn; beginning in first sc, sc2tog, sc in next 5 sc, sc2tog: 7 sc.

Edging: Turn; slip st evenly around entire piece; join with slip st to first slip st, finish off leaving a long end for sewing.

HEAD TUFF

With smaller size hook and White, ch 5.

Row 1 (Right side)**:** (3 Dc, ch 3, slip st) in third ch from hook, (slip st, ch 2, 3 dc, ch 3, slip st) in each of last 2 chs; finish off leaving a long end for sewing.

NOSE

With smaller size hook and Pink, ch 3.

Row 1 (Right side)**:** Sc in second ch from hook and in last ch; finish off leaving a long end for sewing: 2 sc.

EAR (Make 2)

With smaller size hook and Black, ch 7.

Row 1: Sc in second ch from hook, dc in last 5 chs; finish off leaving a long end for sewing.

EYE (Make 2)

Rnd 1 (Right side)**:** With smaller size hook and White, make an adjustable loop to form a ring; 6 sc in ring; join with slip st to first sc, finish off leaving a long end for sewing.

Pupil: With smaller size hook and Black, ch 3; finish off leaving a long end for sewing.

FACE ASSEMBLY

Use photo as a guide for placement of all pieces.

Sew each Pupil to the edge of an Eye at the joining.

Use 🎥 backstitch *(Fig. 7, page 47)* for the method of sewing to attach the features to the Body, leaving the edge of each piece free.

Sew the Head Tuff to the top of the Head.

Sew the Nose to the bottom of the Head.

Sew the Eyes to the Head with the Pupils positioned to one side.

Sew the Ears to the top of the Head, placing the last dc of each Ear across Rows 13-15 of the Head; tack the first sc to Row 10.

Sew the Head to the Body Front at an angle.

FINISHING

The pillow form may be covered if desired.

Place the Front and Back Body pieces with **wrong** sides together and the beginning chs at the same end. Working through **both** layers, join White with slip st in any corner; slip st around to join pieces, inserting the pillow form before working across the last side; join with slip st to first st.

Sew Legs to bottom corners of Body.

Sew the last dc of the Tail to the top corner of the Body.

Hippo

EASY

Finished Size: 12" x 16"
(30.5 cm x 40.5 cm)

Shopping List

Yarn (Medium Weight)

[7 ounces, 370 yards
(198 grams, 338 meters) per skein]:

☐ Purple - 1 skein
☐ Lilac - 36 yards (33 meters)
☐ White - small amount
☐ Black - small amount

Crochet Hooks

☐ Size I (5.5 mm) **and**
☐ Size J (6 mm)
  or sizes needed for gauge

Additional Supplies

☐ Pillow form - 12" x 16"
  (30.5 cm x 40.5 cm)
☐ Yarn needle

GAUGE INFORMATION

The pillow Body is worked with the larger size hook. All other pieces are worked with the smaller size hook.

With larger size hook, in Body pattern,
2 repeats (12 sts) = 4$\frac{1}{2}$" (11.5 cm),
6 rows = 3$\frac{1}{4}$" (8.25 cm)

Gauge Swatch: 5" wide x 3$\frac{1}{4}$" high
(12.75 cm x 8.25 cm)

With larger size hook and Purple,
ch 14.
Work same as Body Rows 1-6:
2 5-dc groups and 2 sc.
Finish off.

—— STITCH GUIDE ——

 TREBLE CROCHET
  (abbreviated tr)

YO twice, insert hook in st indicated, YO and pull up a loop (4 loops on hook), (YO and draw through 2 loops on hook) 3 times.

INSTRUCTIONS

BODY (Make 2)

With larger size hook, Purple, and beginning at bottom edge, ch 38.

Row 1: 5 Dc in fifth ch from hook, skip next 2 chs, sc in next ch, ★ skip next 2 chs, 5 dc in next ch, skip next 2 chs, sc in next ch; repeat from ★ across: 6 5-dc groups and 6 sc.

Row 2: Ch 2, turn; 2 dc in first sc, skip next 2 dc, sc in next dc, ★ skip next 2 dc, 5 dc in next sc, skip next 2 dc, sc in next dc; repeat from ★ across to last 2 dc, skip last 2 dc, 3 dc in next ch: 5 5-dc groups and 6 sc.

Row 3: Ch 1, turn; skip first 3 dc, 5 dc in next sc, ★ skip next 2 dc, sc in next dc, skip next 2 dc, 5 dc in next sc; repeat from ★ across to last 2 dc, skip last 2 dc, sc in next ch: 6 5-dc groups and 6 sc.

Repeat Rows 2 and 3 for pattern until Body measures approximately 16$\frac{1}{4}$" (41.5 cm) from beginning ch.

Finish off leaving a long end for sewing on only one of the Body pieces.

EAR (Make 2)

With smaller size hook and Purple, ch 7.

Row 1 (Right side)**:** 2 Dc in third ch from hook, 2 tr in each of next 3 chs, (2 dc, ch 2, slip st) in last ch; finish off leaving a long end for sewing.

LEG (Make 4)

Rnd 1 (Right side)**:** With smaller size hook and Purple, ▓◀ make an adjustable loop to form a ring *(Figs. 1a-d, page 46)*; ch 1, 12 dc in ring; join with slip st to first dc.

Turning ch-2 does **not** count as a st.

Rnd 2: Ch 2, ▓◀ working in Back Loops Only *(Fig. 4, page 46)*, dc in each dc around; join with slip st to **both** loops of first dc.

Rnd 3: Ch 2, dc in both loops of each dc around; join with slip st to first dc, finish off leaving a long end for sewing.

SNOUT

With smaller size hook and Lilac, ch 14.

Rnd 1 (Right side)**:** 2 Dc in third ch from hook, dc in next 10 chs, 7 dc in last ch; ▓◀ working in free loops of beginning ch *(Fig. 3, page 46)*, dc in next 10 chs, 5 dc in next ch; join with slip st to first dc: 34 dc.

Note: Loop a short piece of yarn around any stitch to mark Rnd 1 as **right** side.

Turning ch-2 does **not** count as a st.

Rnd 2: Ch 2, do **not** turn; 2 dc in same st as joining and in next dc, dc in next 10 dc, 2 dc in each of next 7 dc, dc in next 10 dc, 2 dc in each of last 5 dc; join with slip st to first dc: 48 dc.

Rnd 3: Ch 2, dc in same st as joining, 2 dc in next dc, dc in next dc, 2 dc in next dc, dc in next 11 dc, 2 dc in next dc, (dc in next dc, 2 dc in next dc) 6 times, dc in next 11 dc, 2 dc in next dc, (dc in next dc, 2 dc in next dc) 4 times; join with slip st to first dc: 62 dc.

Rnd 4: Ch 2, dc in same st as joining and in next dc, 2 dc in next dc, dc in next 2 dc, 2 dc in next dc, dc in next 12 dc, 2 dc in next dc, (dc in next 2 dc, 2 dc in next dc) 6 times, dc in next 12 dc, 2 dc in next dc, (dc in next 2 dc, 2 dc in next dc) 4 times; join with slip st to first dc, finish off leaving a long end for sewing: 76 dc.

TOOTH (Make 2)

With smaller size hook and White, ch 4.

Row 1: Sc in second ch from hook and in last 2 chs: 3 sc.

Row 2: Ch 1, turn; sc in each sc across; finish off leaving a long end for sewing.

EYE (Make 2)

Row 1 (Right side)**:** With smaller size hook and White, make an adjustable loop to form a ring; 7 sc in ring; do **not** join.

Row 2: 2 Sc in each of next 7 sc, slip st in next sc; finish off leaving a long end for sewing.

Pupil: With Black, ch 4; join with slip st to form a ring, finish off leaving a long end for sewing.

FACE ASSEMBLY

Use photo as a guide for placement of all pieces.

Sew each Pupil to the edge of an Eye at the joining.

Smile: With smaller size hook and Black, ch 30; finish off leaving a long end for sewing.

With the joining on the Snout facing downward, sew the Smile in place.

Sew the Teeth under the Smile.

Nostril Dot (Make 2)**:** With smaller size hook and Black, ch 3; finish off leaving a long end for sewing.

Sew the Nostril Dots to Rnd 2 of the Snout.

Use 🎥 backstitch *(Fig. 7, page 47)* for the method of sewing to attach the features to the Body, leaving the edge of each piece free.

Sew the Snout to the Body, beginning 4" (10 cm) down from the top edge.

Sew the Eyes to the Body placing the bottom of the Eyes at the top edge of the Snout.

Using Black, sew 3 short sts across the top of each Eye and the Body for eyelashes.

FINISHING

The pillow form may be covered if desired.

Place the Body pieces together with the beginning chs at the same end. 🎥 Whipstitch across each side *(Figs. 6a & b, page 47)*, inserting the pillow form before working across the last side.

Using photo as a guide for placement, flatten Legs and sew to Body at seams.

Fold the beginning ch of the Ears in half and sew them to the top corners of the Body.

Pig

■■□□ EASY

Finished Size: 12" x 16"
(30.5 cm x 40.5 cm)

Shopping List

Yarn (Medium Weight) [4]

[7 ounces, 370 yards
(198 grams, 338 meters) per skein]:

☐ Pink - 1 skein
☐ Rose - 50 yards (45.5 meters)
☐ White - small amount
☐ Brown - small amount

Crochet Hooks

☐ Size I (5.5 mm) **and**
☐ Size J (6 mm)
  or sizes needed for gauge

Additional Supplies

☐ Pillow form - 12" x 16"
  (30.5 cm x 40.5 cm)
☐ Yarn needle

GAUGE INFORMATION

The pillow Body is worked with the larger size hook. All other pieces are worked with the smaller size hook.

With larger size hook, in Body pattern,
  10 sts and 10 rows = 3" (7.5 cm)

Gauge Swatch: 3" (7.5 cm) square
With larger size hook and Pink, ch 12.
Work same as Body Rows 1-10: 5 sc and 5 sps.
Finish off.

STITCH GUIDE

 TREBLE CROCHET
  (abbreviated tr)

YO twice, insert hook in st indicated, YO and pull up a loop (4 loops on hook), (YO and draw through 2 loops on hook) 3 times.

INSTRUCTIONS

The Body is worked across the width of the front and the back. The end of rows will be joined to form a seam lengthwise across the center back.

BODY

With larger size hook Pink, and beginning at bottom edge, ch 92.

Row 1: Sc in fourth ch from hook **(3 skipped chs count as first sp)**, (ch 1, skip next ch, sc in next ch) across: 45 sc and 45 sps.

Row 2: Ch 2 **(counts as first sp)**, turn; (sc in next ch-1 sp, ch 1) across to last sp, sc in last sp.

Repeat Row 2 for pattern until Body measures approximately 16¼" (41.5 cm) from beginning ch.

Finish off leaving a long end for sewing.

Back seam: Fold the Body piece in half matching rows. ▪ Whipstitch across the end of rows **(Fig. 6b, page 47)**.

EAR (Make 2)

With smaller size hook and Pink, ch 9.

Row 1: ▪ Working in back ridge of chs **(Fig. 2, page 46)**, sc in second ch from hook, hdc in next ch, dc in next 2 chs, tr in last 4 chs; finish off leaving a long end for sewing.

LEG (Make 4)

Rnd 1 (Right side)**:** With smaller size hook and Pink, ▪ make an adjustable loop to form a ring **(Figs. 1a-d, page 46)**; 8 sc in ring; do **not** join, ▪ place a marker to indicate beginning of the rnd **(see Markers, page 46)**.

Rnds 2 and 3: Sc in each sc around.

Slip st in next sc, finish off leaving a long end for sewing.

Rnd 8: (2 Sc in next sc, sc in next 6 sc) around: 56 sc.

Rnd 9: (2 Sc in next sc, sc in next 7 sc) around: 63 sc.

Rnd 10: (2 Sc in next sc, sc in next 8 sc) around: 70 sc.

Rnd 11: (2 Sc in next sc, sc in next 9 sc) around: 77 sc.

Rnd 12: (2 Sc in next sc, sc in next 10 sc) around: 84 sc.

Slip st in next sc, finish off leaving a long end for sewing.

TAIL

With smaller size hook and Pink, ch 9.

Row 1: 3 Sc in second ch from hook and in each ch across; finish off leaving a long end for sewing : 24 sc.

Sew the Tail to the Body at the back seam, 4" (10 cm) up from the bottom edge.

TUMMY

Rnd 1 (Right side)**:** With smaller size hook and Rose, make an adjustable loop to form a ring; 7 sc in ring; do **not** join, place a marker to indicate beginning of the rnd.

Note: Loop a short piece of yarn around any stitch to mark Rnd 1 as **right** side.

Rnd 2: 2 Sc in each sc around: 14 sc.

Rnd 3: (2 Sc in next sc, sc in next sc) around: 21 sc.

Rnd 4: (2 Sc in next sc, sc in next 2 sc) around: 28 sc.

Rnd 5: (2 Sc in next sc, sc in next 3 sc) around: 35 sc.

Rnd 6: (2 Sc in next sc, sc in next 4 sc) around: 42 sc.

Rnd 7: (2 Sc in next sc, sc in next 5 sc) around: 49 sc.

SNOUT

With smaller size hook and Rose, ch 7.

Rnd 1 (Right side)**:** 3 Sc in second ch from hook, sc in next 4 chs, 3 sc in last ch; 🎥 working in free loops of beginning ch **(Fig. 3, page 46)**, sc in next 4 chs; join with slip st to first sc: 14 sc.

Note: Mark Rnd 1 as **right** side.

Rnd 2: Ch 1, do **not** turn; 2 sc in same st as joining and in each of next 2 sc, sc in next 4 sc, 2 sc in each of next 3 sc, sc in last 4 sc; join with slip st to first sc: 20 sc.

Rnd 3: Ch 1, sc in same st as joining, 2 sc in next sc, (sc in next sc, 2 sc in next sc) twice, sc in next 5 sc, 2 sc in next sc, (sc in next sc, 2 sc in next sc) twice, sc in last 4 sc; join with slip st to first sc, finish off leaving a long end for sewing: 26 sc.

EYE (Make 2)

Rnd 1 (Right side)**:** With smaller size hook and White, make an adjustable loop to form a ring; 6 sc in ring; join with slip st to first sc, finish off leaving a long end for sewing.

Pupil: With Brown, ch 3; finish off leaving a long end for sewing.

FACE ASSEMBLY

Use photo as a guide for placement of all pieces.

Sew each Pupil to the edge of an Eye at the joining.

Nostril Dot (Make 2)**:** With smaller size hook and Pink, ch 3; finish off leaving a long end for sewing.

Sew the Nostril Dots to the Snout.

Flatten the Body with the seam at the side edge and mark the top and bottom edges of the fold to indicate the center of the front.

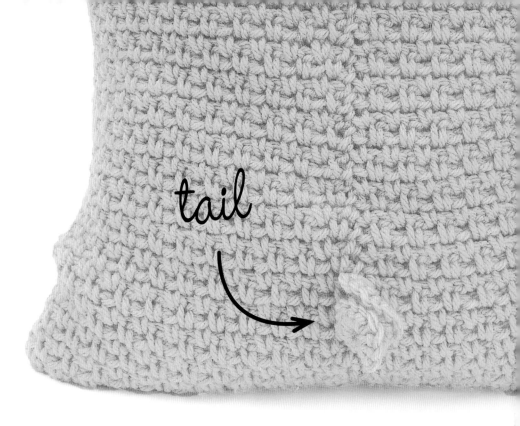

tail

Use backstitch *(Fig. 7, page 47)* for the method of sewing to attach the features to the Body, leaving the edge of each piece free.

Move the seam to the center back. Using the markers as a guide, place the Snout on the front of the Body, beginning 4" (10 cm) down from the top edge and sew in place.

Sew the Eyes to the Body, placing the bottom of the Eyes at the top edge of the Snout with the Pupils positioned slightly to one side.

FINISHING

The pillow form may be covered if desired.

The pillow form can be temporarily inserted at any time to make placement of pieces easier.

Sew the Tummy to the front of the Body.

Sew the Legs to the Body.

Sew the Ears to the Body across the last tr, 1" (2.5 cm) from the top edge.

Remove the pillow form to weave in the yarn ends.

Flatten the Body placing the seam and bottom marker together; whipstitch across the bottom edge *(Fig. 6a, page 47)*.

Insert the pillow form. Flatten the top edge of the Body placing the seam and top marker together, then whipstitch across the top edge.

Panda

■■□□ EASY

Finished Size: 12" x 16"
(30.5 cm x 40.5 cm)

Shopping List

Yarn (Medium Weight)

[7 ounces, 370 yards
(198 grams, 338 meters) per skein]:

☐ Black - 1 skein

☐ White - 1 skein

☐ Rose - small amount

Crochet Hooks

☐ Size I (5.5 mm) **and**

☐ Size J (6 mm)

or sizes needed for gauge

Additional Supplies

☐ Pillow form - 12" x 16"
(30.5 cm x 40.5 cm)

☐ Yarn needle

GAUGE INFORMATION

The pillow Body and Head are worked with the larger size hook. All other pieces are worked with the smaller size hook.

With larger size hook, in Body pattern,
10 sts and 10 rows = 3" (7.5 cm)

Gauge Swatch: 3" (7.5 cm) square

With larger size hook and Black, ch 12.

Work same as Body Rows 1-10: 5 sc and 5 sps.

Finish off.

——— STITCH GUIDE ———

📹◄ DOUBLE CROCHET 2 TOGETHER
(abbreviated dc2tog) (uses 2 sts)
★ YO, insert hook in **next** st, YO and pull up a loop, YO and draw through 2 loops on hook; repeat from ★ once **more**, YO and draw through all 3 loops on hook (**counts as one dc**).

INSTRUCTIONS

The Body and Head are worked across the width of the front and the back. The end of rows will be joined to form a seam across the center back.

BODY

With larger size hook, Black, and beginning at bottom edge, ch 92.

Row 1 (Right side)**:** Sc in fourth ch from hook (**3 skipped chs count as first sp**), (ch 1, skip next ch, sc in next ch) across: 45 sc and 45 sps.

Note: Loop a short piece of yarn around any stitch to mark Row 1 as **right** side.

Row 2: Ch 2 (**counts as first sp**), turn; (sc in next ch-1 sp, ch 1) across to last sp, sc in last sp.

Repeat Row 2 for pattern until Body measures approximately 8" (20.5 cm) from beginning ch, ending by working a **wrong** side row; finish off leaving a long end for sewing.

HEAD

Row 1: With **right** side facing, join White with slip st in first sc; slip st in each ch and in each sc across: 90 sts.

Row 2: Ch 2, turn; skip first st, **📹◄** working in Front Loops Only (*Fig. 4, page 46*), sc in next st, (ch 1, skip next st, sc in next st) across: 45 sc and 45 sps.

Row 3: Ch 2, turn; (sc in next ch-1 sp, ch 1) across to last sp, sc in last sp.

Repeat Row 3 for pattern until piece measures approximately 16¼" (41.5 cm) from beginning ch.

Finish off leaving a long end for sewing.

Back seam: Fold the Body piece in half with **wrong** side together and matching rows. 📹 Whipstitch across the end of rows *(Fig. 6b, page 47)* using matching yarn.

EAR (Make 2)

Row 1: With smaller size hook and Black, 📹 make an adjustable loop to form a ring *(Figs. 1a-d, page 46)*; (2 sc, 4 dc, 2 sc) in ring; do **not** join: 8 sts.

Row 2 (Right side)**:** Ch 1, turn; sc in first 2 sc, 2 sc in each of next 4 dc, sc in last 2 sc; finish off leaving a long end for sewing: 12 sc.

Note: Mark Row 2 as **right** side.

LEG (Make 4)

Rnd 1 (Right side)**:** With smaller size hook and Black, make an adjustable loop to form a ring; 6 sc in ring; join with slip st to first sc, finish off leaving a long end for sewing.

FIRST EYE PATCH

Rnd 1 (Right side)**:** With smaller size hook and Black, make an adjustable loop to form a ring; 7 sc in ring; join with slip st to first sc.

Note: Mark Rnd 1 as **right** side.

Rnd 2: Ch 9, sc in second ch from hook and in next 7 chs, 2 sc in each of next 7 sc; 📹 working in free loops of ch *(Fig. 3, page 46)*, skip next ch, slip st in next 7 chs, (slip st, ch 1) twice in last ch; do **not** join.

Rnd 3: Sc in next sc, hdc in next 2 sc, dc in next 7 sc, 2 dc in each of next 9 sc, dc in next sc, dc2tog, skip next 3 sts, slip st in next 4 sts; finish off leaving a long end for sewing.

SECOND EYE PATCH

Rnd 1 (Right side)**:** With smaller size hook and Black, make an adjustable loop to form a ring; 7 sc in ring; join with slip st to first sc.

Note: Mark Rnd 1 as **right** side.

Rnd 2: Ch 9, slip st in second ch from hook and in next 6 chs, skip last ch, 2 sc in each of next 7 sc; working in free loops of ch, sc in next 8 chs, (ch 1, slip st) twice in last ch; do **not** join.

Rnd 3: Slip st in next 4 sts, skip next 3 sts, dc2tog, dc in next sc, 2 dc in each of next 9 sc, dc in next 7 sc, hdc in next 2 sc, sc in last sc, slip st in next st; finish off leaving a long end for sewing.

EYE (Make 2)

Rnd 1 (Right side)**:** With smaller size hook and White, make an adjustable loop to form a ring; 6 sc in ring; join with slip st to first sc, finish off leaving a long end for sewing.

Pupil: With Black, ch 3; finish off leaving a long end for sewing.

NOSE & MOUTH

With smaller size hook and Black, make an adjustable loop to form a ring; 6 sc in ring; join with slip st to first sc; ch 16; finish off leaving a long end for sewing.

CHEEK (Make 2)

Rnd 1 (Right side)**:** With smaller size hook and Rose, make an adjustable loop to form a ring; 9 sc in ring; join with slip st to first sc, finish off leaving a long end for sewing.

FACE ASSEMBLY

Use photo as a guide for placement of all pieces.

Sew each Pupil to the edge of an Eye at the joining.

Use  backstitch *(Fig. 7, page 47)* for the method of sewing to attach the features to the Body, leaving the edge of each piece free.

Sew each Eye to an Eye Patch with the Pupils positioned slightly to one side.

Flatten the Body and Head with the seam at the side edge and mark the top and bottom edges of the fold to indicate the center of the front.

Move the seam to the center back. Using the markers as a guide, place the Eye Patches on the front of the Head, beginning 1½" (4 cm) down from the top edge and 1" (2.5 cm) apart; sew in place.

Sew the Cheeks to the Head under the curve of the Eye Patches.

Sew the Nose to the Head, then sew the first 4 chs straight down. Fold the remaining chs to form the mouth, placing 3 chs to one side, 6 chs across the bottom, and 3 chs to the other side and sew in place.

FINISHING

The pillow form may be covered if desired.

The pillow form can be temporarily inserted at any time to make placement of pieces easier.

Sew 2 Legs to the bottom front corners of the Body and 2 Legs at the color change.

Sew the straight edge of the Ears to the top front corners of the Head.

Remove the pillow form to weave in the yarn ends.

Flatten the Body placing the seam and bottom marker together; whipstitch across the bottom edge *(Fig. 6a, page 47)*.

Insert the pillow form. Flatten the top edge of the Head placing the seam and top marker together, then whipstitch across the top edge.

Bee

■■□□ EASY

Finished Size: 12" x 16"
(30.5 cm x 40.5 cm)

Shopping List

Yarn (Medium Weight)

[7 ounces, 370 yards
(198 grams, 338 meters) per skein]:

- ☐ Yellow - 1 skein
- ☐ Black - 75 yards (68.5 meters)
- ☐ White - 30 yards (27.5 meters)
- ☐ Pink - small amount
- ☐ Rose - small amount

Crochet Hooks

- ☐ Size I (5.5 mm) **and**
- ☐ Size J (6 mm)
  or sizes needed for gauge

Additional Supplies

- ☐ Pillow form - 12" x 16"
  (30.5 cm x 40.5 cm)
- ☐ Yarn needle

GAUGE INFORMATION

The pillow Body is worked with the larger size hook. All other pieces are worked with the smaller size hook.

With larger size hook, in strip pattern,
 11 sts = 4" (10 cm),
 7 rnds = 2¾" (7 cm)

Gauge Swatch: 4" wide x 2¾" high
 (10 cm x 7 cm)

With larger size hook and Yellow, ch 22; being careful **not** to twist ch, join with slip st to form a ring.
Work same as Body Rnds 1-7: 22 sts. Finish off.

——— STITCH GUIDE ———

TREBLE CROCHET

 (abbreviated tr)

YO twice, insert hook in st indicated, YO and pull up a loop (4 loops on hook), (YO and draw through 2 loops on hook) 3 times.

SINGLE CROCHET 2 TOGETHER

 (abbreviated sc2tog) (uses 2 sc)

Pull up a loop in each of next 2 sc, YO and draw through all 3 loops on hook **(counts as one sc)**.

CHANGING COLORS

To change colors while joining a round with a slip stitch, drop the yarn to the **wrong** side, insert hook in first stitch, hook new yarn and draw through stitch and loop on hook **(Fig. A)**.

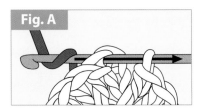

Fig. A

INSTRUCTIONS

The Body is worked in rounds around the width of the front and the back. The **wrong** side (inside of the pillow) will be facing you as you work.

BODY

With larger size hook, Yellow, and beginning at bottom edge, ch 72; being careful **not** to twist ch, join with slip st to form a ring.

Rnd 1 (Wrong side)**:** Ch 2 **(counts as first hdc, now and throughout)**, hdc in next ch and in each ch around; join with slip st to first hdc: 72 hdc.

Rnds 2-4: Ch 2, do **not** turn; hdc in next hdc and in each hdc around; join with slip st to first hdc.

Rnd 5: Ch 2, hdc in next hdc and in each hdc around; drop Yellow to the front, with Black, join with slip st to first hdc **(Fig. A)**.

Rnd 6: Ch 1, sc in each hdc around; join with slip st to first sc.

Rnd 7: Ch 1, sc in each sc around; cut Black, with Yellow, join with slip st to first sc.

Rnds 8-11: Ch 2, hdc in next st and in each st around; join with slip st to first hdc.

Rnd 12: Ch 2, hdc in next hdc and in each hdc around; drop Yellow to the front, with Black, join with slip st to first hdc.

Rnds 13-28: Repeat Rnds 6-12 twice, then repeat Rnds 6 and 7 once **more**.

Repeat Rnd 8 until Body measures approximately 16¼" (41.5 cm) from beginning ch.

Finish off leaving a long end for sewing.

WING (Make 2)

With smaller size hook and White, ch 4.

Row 1: Sc in second ch from hook and in last 2 chs: 3 sc.

Row 2: Ch 2, turn; 2 sc in second ch from hook and in next sc, sc in next sc, 2 sc in last sc: 7 sc.

Row 3: Ch 1, turn; sc in first 6 sc, 2 sc in last sc: 8 sc.

Rows 4-6: Ch 1, turn; sc in each sc across.

Row 7 (Decrease row)**:** Ch 1, turn; sc in each sc across to last 2 sc, sc2tog: 7 sc.

Row 8 (Decrease row)**:** Ch 1, turn; beginning in first sc, sc2tog, sc in each sc across: 6 sc.

Rows 9 and 10: Repeat Rows 7 and 8: 4 sc.

Row 11: Ch 1, turn; sc in first 2 sc, leave remaining 2 sc unworked: 2 sc.

Row 12: Ch 3, turn; sc in second ch from hook and in next ch, sc in last 2 sc: 4 sc.

Row 13 (Increase row)**:** Ch 1, turn; sc in first 3 sc, 2 sc in last sc: 5 sc.

Row 14 (Increase row)**:** Ch 1, turn; 2 sc in first sc, sc in each sc across: 6 sc.

Rows 15 and 16: Repeat Rows 13 and 14: 8 sc.

Rows 17 and 18: Ch 1, turn; sc in each sc across.

Row 19: Ch 1, turn; sc in each sc across to last 2 sc, sc2tog: 7 sc.

Row 20: Turn; slip st in first sc, sc2tog, sc in last 4 sc: 5 sc.

Row 21: Ch 1, turn; beginning in first sc, sc2tog, sc in next sc, sc2tog: 3 sc.

The Edging denotes the **right** side. Each Wing will have the Edging worked on the opposite side allowing the Wings to match.

First Wing Edging (Right side)**:** Turn; slip st evenly around entire Wing; join with slip st to first slip st, finish off leaving a long end for sewing.

Note: Loop a short piece of yarn around stitch **below** last stitch made to mark Edging as **right** side and joining as top edge.

Second Wing Edging (Right side)**:** Do **not** turn; slip st evenly around entire Wing; join with slip st to first slip st, finish off leaving a long end for sewing.

Note: Mark Edging as **right** side and joining as top edge.

STINGER

With smaller size hook and Black, ch 10.

Row 1: Slip st in second ch from hook, sc in next 2 chs, hdc in next 2 chs, dc in next 2 chs, tr in last 2 chs: 9 sts.

Row 2: Ch 3, turn; skip first tr, tr in next tr, dc in next 2 dc, hdc in next 2 hdc, sc in next 2 sc, slip st in last slip st; finish off leaving a long end for sewing.

stinger

ANTENNA (Make 2)

With smaller size hook and Black, ch 9; 5 sc in second ch from hook; join with slip st to first sc, slip st in last 7 chs; finish off leaving a long end for sewing.

EYE (Make 2)

With smaller size hook and Black, ch 4; join with slip st to form a ring, finish off leaving a long end for sewing.

CHEEK (Make 2)

Rnd 1 (Right side): With smaller size hook and Pink, 🎥 make an adjustable loop to form a ring *(Figs. 1a-d, page 46)*; 9 sc in ring; join with slip st to first sc, finish off leaving a long end for sewing.

FACE ASSEMBLY

Use photo as a guide for placement of all pieces.

The joining of the third Black stripe will be the center back of the pillow. Flatten the Body with this joining placed at the side edge and mark the top and bottom edges of the opposite fold to indicate the center of the front.

Smile: With smaller size hook and Rose, ch 6; finish off leaving a long end for sewing.

Move the joinings to the back. Using the markers as a guide, sew the Eyes and the Smile to the front of the Body, centered from side to side on the top Yellow stripe.

Use 🎥 backstitch *(Fig. 7, page 47)* for the method of sewing to attach the features to the Body, leaving the edge of each piece free.

Sew the Cheeks to the front of the Body.

FINISHING

The pillow form may be covered if desired.

Flatten the Body being sure the face is centered on the front; 🎥 whipstitch across the top edge *(Fig. 6b, page 47)*.

Sew the Antennae to the top seam.

The pillow form can be temporarily inserted in the Body to make placement of the Wings easier. With the **right** side of the Wings facing and the markers at the top, sew the straight edge to the Body.

Fold the Stinger in half and sew the stitches on Row 2 to the beginning ch; sew the wide end across Rnds 9 and 10 of center back, 4" (10 cm) up from the bottom edge.

Remove the pillow form to weave in the yarn ends.

Insert the pillow form. Flatten the bottom edge of the Body, then whipstitch across the bottom edge.

Penguin

EASY

Finished Size: 12" x 16"
(30.5 cm x 40.5 cm)

Shopping List

Yarn (Medium Weight)

[7 ounces, 370 yards
(198 grams, 338 meters) per skein]:

☐ Black - 1 skein

☐ White - 1 skein

☐ Yellow - small amount

☐ Pink - small amount

Crochet Hooks

☐ Size I (5.5 mm) **and**

☐ Size J (6 mm)

or sizes needed for gauge

Additional Supplies

☐ Pillow form - 12" x 16"
(30.5 cm x 40.5 cm)

☐ Yarn needle

GAUGE INFORMATION

The pillow Front and Back Body are worked with the larger size hook. All other pieces are worked with the smaller size hook.

With larger size hook,

11 hdc and 9 rows = 4" (10 cm),

11 sc and 13 rows = 4" (10 cm)

Gauge Swatch: 4" (10 cm) square

With larger size hook and White, ch 13.

Row 1: Hdc in third ch from hook and in each ch across: 11 hdc.

Turning ch-2 does **not** count as a st.

Rows 2-9: Ch 2, turn; hdc in each hdc across.

Finish off.

STITCH GUIDE

TREBLE CROCHET

(abbreviated tr)

YO twice, insert hook in st indicated, YO and pull up a loop (4 loops on hook), (YO and draw through 2 loops on hook) 3 times.

DOUBLE CROCHET 2 TOGETHER

(abbreviated dc2tog) (uses 2 sts)

★ YO, insert hook in **next** st, YO and pull up a loop, YO and draw through 2 loops on hook; repeat from ★ once **more**, YO and draw through all 3 loops on hook (**counts as one dc**).

CLUSTER (uses one sc)

★ YO twice, insert hook in sc indicated, YO and pull up a loop, (YO and draw through 2 loops on hook) twice; repeat from ★ once **more**, YO and draw through all 3 loops on hook.

INSTRUCTIONS
FRONT BODY

With larger size hook, White, beginning at bottom edge, and leaving a long end for sewing, ch 39.

Row 1: Hdc in third ch from hook and in each ch across: 37 hdc.

Turning ch-2 does **not** count as a st.

Row 2: Ch 2, turn; hdc in each hdc across.

Repeat Row 2 until Front Body measures approximately 16¼" (41.5 cm) from beginning ch.

Finish off.

BACK BODY

With larger size hook, Black, beginning at bottom edge, and leaving a long end for sewing, ch 35.

Row 1: Sc in second ch from hook and in each ch across: 34 sc.

Row 2: Ch 1, turn; sc in each sc across.

Repeat Row 2 until Back Body measures approximately 16¼" (41.5 cm) from beginning ch.

Finish off.

Body Seam: Place the Front and Back Body pieces together with the beginning chs at the same end. Using the long end left at the beginning of the Back, 🎥 whipstitch across the side, top, and second side edges *(Figs. 6a & b, page 47)*. Leave the bottom edge unjoined.

HEAD PIECE (Make 2)

The Head Piece is made in two identical halves. The last row of each half will be sewn together to form the center point.

With smaller size hook, Black, and leaving a long end for sewing, ch 23.

Row 1: Sc in second ch from hook and in each ch across: 22 sc.

Row 2: Turn; slip st in first sc, sc in next 2 sc, hdc in next 2 sc, dc in last 17 sc.

Turning ch-2 does **not** count as a st.

Row 3: Ch 2, turn; dc in first 10 dc, hdc in next 2 dc, sc in next dc, slip st in next dc, leave remaining 8 sts unworked: 14 sts.

Row 4: Turn; skip first slip st, slip st in next 3 sts, sc in next dc, hdc in next dc, dc in last 8 dc: 13 sts.

Row 5: Ch 2, turn; dc in first 8 dc, leave remaining 5 sts unworked.

Row 6: Turn; slip st in first dc, sc in next dc, dc in last 6 dc.

Row 7: Ch 2, turn; dc in first 5 dc, dc2tog, leave remaining slip st unworked: 6 dc.

Rows 8 and 9: Ch 2, turn; dc in each dc across.

Row 10: Ch 2, turn; 2 dc in first dc, dc in last 5 dc: 7 dc.

Row 11: Ch 1, turn; sc in each dc across.

Row 12: Ch 3, turn; sc in second ch from hook and in next ch, sc in last 7 sc; finish off leaving a long end for sewing: 9 sc.

Use photo as a guide for placement of all pieces.

Place the Head Pieces together, matching shape and sts on Row 12. Whipstitch pieces together; do **not** cut yarn.

Use 🎥 backstitch *(Fig. 7, page 47)* for the method of sewing to attach the features to the Body, unless otherwise specified, leaving the edge of each piece free.

Place the Head Piece on the Front Body, matching the straight edge to the top seam of the Body. Using the long end left at the end of Row 12 at the straight edge, whipstitch the outer edge of the Head Piece to the Body. Use backstitch to sew around the inner edge, switching to the long end left at the point if needed, then whipstitch the remaining outer edge to the Body.

WING (Make 2)

With smaller size hook and Black, ch 20.

Row 1 (Right side)**:** Tr in fourth ch from hook and in next 7 chs, dc in next 5 chs, hdc in next 2 chs, sc in next ch, 3 sc in last ch; 🎥 working in free loops of beginning ch *(Fig. 3, page 46)*, sc in next ch, hdc in next 2 chs, dc in next 5 chs, tr in next 7 chs, (tr, ch 2, slip st) in next ch; finish off leaving a long end for sewing.

Sew the end of Row 1 of Wings to end of rows on Head Piece; tack beginning ch of Wing across 5 sts to Front Body.

HEAD TUFF

With smaller size hook, join Black with slip st around before the center top of Front Body; (ch 11, slip st around next st) 3 times; finish off.

FOOT (Make 2)

With smaller size hook and Yellow, ch 6.

Row 1 (Right side): Sc in second ch from hook and in each ch across: 5 sc.

Note: Loop a short piece of yarn around any stitch to mark Row 1 as **right** side.

Row 2: Ch 1, turn; 2 sc in first sc, sc in next 3 sc, 2 sc in last sc: 7 sc.

Row 3: Turn; slip st in first sc, ★ ch 3, work Cluster in next sc, ch 3, slip st in next sc; repeat from ★ 2 times **more**; finish off leaving a long end for sewing.

BEAK

With smaller size hook and Yellow, ch 6.

Row 1 (Right side): Dc in third ch from hook, tr in next ch, dc in next ch, ch 2, slip st in last ch; finish off leaving a long end for sewing.

EYE (Make 2)

With smaller size hook and Black, ch 4; join with slip st to form a ring, finish off leaving a long end for sewing.

CHEEK (Make 2)

With smaller size hook and Pink, 🎥 make an adjustable loop to form a ring *(Figs. 1a-d, page 46)*; 9 sc in ring; join with slip st to first sc, finish off leaving a long end for sewing.

FACE ASSEMBLY

Sew the Eyes and the Cheeks to the Front Body. Sew the Beak to the Front Body with the beginning ch at the top.

FINISHING

The pillow form may be covered if desired.

Insert the pillow form, then whipstitch across the bottom edge.

Place each Foot on the Front Body, matching beginning chs; sew around the entire Foot.

General Instructions

ABBREVIATIONS

BPdc	Back Post double crochet(s)
ch(s)	chain(s)
cm	centimeters
dc	double crochet(s)
dc2tog	double crochet 2 together
FPdc	Front Post double crochet(s)
hdc	half double crochet(s)
mm	millimeters
Rnd(s)	Round(s)
sc	single crochet(s)
sc2tog	single crochet 2 together
sp(s)	space(s)
st(s)	stitch(es)
tr	treble crochet(s)
YO	yarn over

SYMBOLS & TERMS

★ — work instructions following ★ as many **more** times as indicated in addition to the first time.

( ) or [ ] — work enclosed instructions **as many** times as specified by the number immediately following **or** work all enclosed instructions in the stitch or space indicated **or** contains explanatory remarks.

colon (:) — the number(s) given after a colon at the end of a row or round denote(s) the number of stitches or spaces you should have on that row or round.

GAUGE

Exact gauge is **essential** for proper size. Before beginning your project, make the sample swatch given in the individual instructions in the yarn and hook specified. After completing the swatch, measure it, counting your stitches and rows or rounds carefully. If your swatch is larger or smaller than specified, **make another, changing hook size to get the correct gauge.** Keep trying until you find the size hook that will give you the specified gauge.

CROCHET TERMINOLOGY

UNITED STATES		INTERNATIONAL
slip stitch (slip st)	=	single crochet (sc)
single crochet (sc)	=	double crochet (dc)
half double crochet (hdc)	=	half treble crochet (htr)
double crochet (dc)	=	treble crochet (tr)
treble crochet (tr)	=	double treble crochet (dtr)
double treble crochet (dtr)	=	triple treble crochet (ttr)
triple treble crochet (tr tr)	=	quadruple treble crochet (qtr)
skip	=	miss

Yarn Weight Symbol & Names	LACE 0	SUPER FINE 1	FINE 2	LIGHT 3	MEDIUM 4	BULKY 5	SUPER BULKY 6
Type of Yarns in Category	Fingering, 10-count crochet thread	Sock, Fingering Baby	Sport, Baby	DK, Light Worsted	Worsted, Afghan, Aran	Chunky, Craft, Rug	Bulky, Roving
Crochet Gauge* Ranges in Single Crochet to 4" (10 cm)	32-42 double crochets**	21-32 sts	16-20 sts	12-17 sts	11-14 sts	8-11 sts	5-9 sts
Advised Hook Size Range	Steel*** 6,7,8 Regular hook B-1	B-1 to E-4	E-4 to 7	7 to I-9	I-9 to K-10½	K-10½ to M/N-13	M/N-13 and larger

*GUIDELINES ONLY: The chart above reflects the most commonly used gauges and hook sizes for specific yarn categories.

** Lace weight yarns are usually crocheted on larger-size hooks to create lacy openwork patterns. Accordingly, a gauge range is difficult to determine. Always follow the gauge stated in your pattern.

*** Steel crochet hooks are sized differently from regular hooks–the higher the number the smaller the hook, which is the reverse of regular hook sizing.

◼◻◻◻ **BEGINNER**	Projects for first-time crocheters using basic stitches. Minimal shaping.	
◼◼◻◻ **EASY**	Projects using yarn with basic stitches, repetitive stitch patterns, simple color changes, and simple shaping and finishing.	
◼◼◼◻ **INTERMEDIATE**	Projects using a variety of techniques, such as basic lace patterns or color patterns, mid-level shaping and finishing.	
◼◼◼◼ **EXPERIENCED**	Projects with intricate stitch patterns, techniques and dimension, such as non-repeating patterns, multi-color techniques, fine threads, small hooks, detailed shaping and refined finishing.	

CROCHET HOOKS																
U.S.	B-1	C-2	D-3	E-4	F-5	G-6	7	H-8	I-9	J-10	K-10½	L-11	M/N-13	N/P-15	P/Q	Q	S
Metric - mm	2.25	2.75	3.25	3.5	3.75	4	4.5	5	5.5	6	6.5	8	9	10	15	16	19

ADJUSTABLE LOOP

Wind the yarn around two fingers to form a ring *(Fig. 1a)*, slide the yarn off your fingers and grasp the strands at the top of the ring *(Fig. 1b)*. Insert the hook from **front** to **back** into the ring, pull up a loop, YO and draw through the loop on hook to lock the ring *(Fig. 1c)*.

Working around **both** strands, work stitches in the ring as specified, then pull the yarn end to close *(Fig. 1d)*.

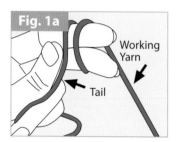

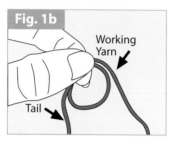

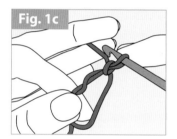

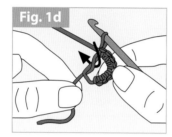

BACK RIDGE

Work only in loops indicated by arrows *(Fig. 2)*.

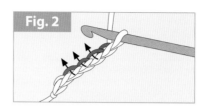

MARKERS

Markers are used to help distinguish the beginning of each round being worked. Place a 2" (5 cm) scrap piece of yarn before the first stitch of each round, moving the marker after each round is complete.

FREE LOOPS OF A CHAIN

When instructed to work in free loops of a chain, work in loop indicated by arrow *(Fig. 3)*.

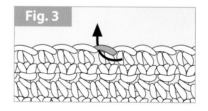

BACK OR FRONT LOOP ONLY

Work only in loop(s) indicated by arrow *(Fig. 4)*.

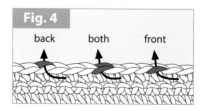

CHANGING COLORS

Work the last stitch to within one step of completion (2 loops on hook), drop yarn, hook new yarn *(Figs. 5a or b)* and draw through both loops on hook. Do **not** cut yarn until indicated.

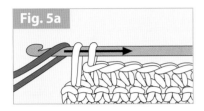

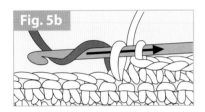

WHIPSTITCH

With **wrong** sides together, sew through both pieces once to secure the beginning of the seam, leaving an ample yarn end to weave in later. Insert the needle from **back** to **front** through **both** loops of each stitch on **both** pieces *(Fig. 6a)*, **or** in end of rows *(Fig. 6b)*. Bring the needle around and insert it from **back** to **front** through the next strands on both pieces.
Continue in same manner, keeping the sewing yarn fairly loose.

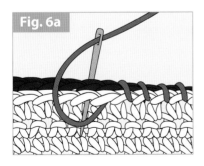

EMBROIDERY STITCHES
BACKSTITCH

Thread a yarn needle with the long yarn end left when finishing off.
Beginning at the edge of the feature, come up at 1, go down at 2 and come up at 3 *(Fig. 7)*. The second stitch is made by going down at 1 and coming up at 4. Continue in the same manner; secure end.

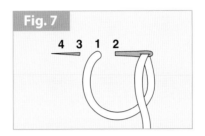

RUNNING STITCH

Running stitch is a series of straight stitches that weaves in and out of the fabric. It is used on the Lion as a temporary stitch to indicated the placement of the Mane. Come up at 1, go down at 2, come up at 3, and go down at 4 *(Fig. 8)*. Continue in the same manner.

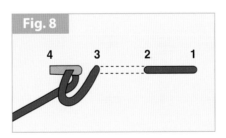

Yarn Information

The pillows in this book were made using Red Heart® With Love®, a medium weight yarn. Any brand of medium weight yarn may be used. It is best to refer to the yardage/meters when determining how many skeins or balls to purchase. Remember, to arrive at the finished size, it is the GAUGE/TENSION that is important, not the brand of yarn.

For your convenience, listed below are the colors used to create our photography models.

FOX
Orange - #1252 Mango
Aran - #1303 Aran
Brown - #1321 Chocolate
Tan - #1308 Tan
Maroon - #1915 Merlot

LION
Gold - #1207 Cornsilk
Orange - #1252 Mango
Brown - #1321 Chocolate
White - #1001 White
Maroon - #1915 Merlot

OWL
Tan - #1308 Tan
Blue - #1805 Bluebell
Yellow - #1201 Daffodil
Orange - #1252 Mango
White - #1001 White
Brown - #1321 Chocolate

MONKEY
Brown - #1321 Chocolate
Tan - #1308 Tan
Rose - #1701 Hot Pink
White - #1001 White
Black - #1012 Black

SHEEP
White - #1001 White
Grey - #1401 Pewter
Black - #1012 Black
Pink - #1704 Bubblegum

HIPPO
Purple - #1542 Aubergine
Lilac - #1538 Lilac
White - #1001 White
Black - #1012 Black

PIG
Pink - #1704 Bubblegum
Rose - #1701 Hot Pink
White - #1001 White
Brown - #1321 Chocolate

PANDA
Black - #1012 Black
White - #1001 White
Rose - #1701 Hot Pink

BEE
Yellow - #1201 Daffodil
Black - #1012 Black
White - #1001 White
Pink - #1704 Bubblegum
Rose - #1701 Hot Pink

PENGUIN
Black - #1012 Black
White - #1001 White
Yellow - #1201 Daffodil
Pink - #1704 Bubblegum